Short-Term Mission Team Essentials — TOGETHER ON THE JOURNEY

LEADER'S GUIDE

"A heart of gratitude goes to the Global Servants, IM's host-country partners, and Associates and Special Assistants to the Short-Term Mission office at International Ministries, who also contributed to this guide."

Prepared by Rev. Dr. Ann E. C. Borquist

Edited by Rev. Sandra Dorsainvil

Graphic design by Devon Nassif

ISBN: 978-1-09833-483-3

All quotations from Scripture are from the New International Version, unless otherwise noted.

International Mnistries, also know as the American Baptist Foreign Missionary Society is the oldest Baptist mission agency formed in North America (formed in 1814). We serve more than over 900 short-term and long-term missionaries annually, bringing U.S. and Puerto Rico churches together with partners in 76 countries in cutting-edge ministries that tell the good news of Jesus Christ while meeting human needs.

International Ministries, 1003 W., 9th Avenue, King of Prussia, PA 19406

Short-Term Mission (STM) Team Essentials —
TOGETHER ON THE JOURNEY

Overview of the STM Essentials Training Guide

Before the First Team Session

A QUICK LOOK AT STM ESSENTIALS GUIDE

Preparation: Before the First Team Session

Session 1: Together on the Journey

Session 2: Cross-Cultural Relationship Building

Session 3: Love One Another

The "STM Team Essentials — Together on the Journey" leader's guide is a step-by-step experiential training program for group training sessions before (Pre-Trip), during (In Country) and after (Post-Trip) your Short-Term Mission experience.

Pre-Trip Training: *Preparing Your Short-Term Mission Team*
(3 sessions)

Devotional material, experiential training exercises and information, logistical information and handouts. (3 Sessions)

Preparation: Before the First Team Session

Session 1: Together on the Journey

Session 2: Cross-Cultural Relationship Building

Session 3: Love One Another

*God's New Thing: An **In-Country Devotional and Reflection Guide*** *for Short Term Mission Teams (10 Days)*

Ideas for reflection, worship and fellowship, including cross-cultural appreciation tips and suggestions for health and safety.

About this Team Devotional Guide

Day 1 – We're here! PTL!

Day 2 – God's New Thing

Day 3 – On the Journey Together

Day 4 – Attitude check

Day 5 – The Gift of Receiving

Day 6 – Giving to Do No Harm

Day 7 – Cracked and broken

Day 8 – On Wings like Eagles

Day 9 – Saying Excellent Good-byes

Day 10 – Celebrate!

On-site briefing topics

International Ministries ABCUSA *works cross-culturally to invite people to become disciples of Jesus Christ and to proclaim, through both word and deed, God's reign of justice, peace and abundant life for all creation.*

Post-Trip Reflection & Action: *Transforming Your Short-Term Experience into Long-Term Action (1 session)*

Debriefing, reflection and discovering how to apply what you have learned "over there" to "here at home." What lessons or skills have you learned that can be shared in your own setting? What "take-aways" could be adapted to teaching-learning opportuntities in your sending church? How has God spoken to you in new ways during this short-term mission experience?

Post-Trip Session:
Looking Back – Sharing the story
Looking Forward – How can this trip lead to lasting change?
What new behavior have you adopted since the mission trip?

Photo by Daniel Buttry

HOW TO
USE "STM
ESSENTIALS —
TOGETHER ON
THE JOURNEY"
TO PREPARE
YOUR SHORT-
TERM MISSION
TEAM

God is preparing an extraordinary experience for you and your Short-Term Mission (STM) team, one that will literally transform your lives. Be prepared for God to work *in, on* and *through* you as you go on this journey.

Now may the Lord of peace himself give you peace at all times and in every way. The Lord be with all of you. 2 Thess. 3:16

STM Team Essentials — Together on the Journey: A Short-Term Mission Team Leader's Guide will guide you through your adventure of participating in God's mission in the world. If you are like most STM leaders, you probably have 101 things on your "to do" list and too few hours in the day to get them all done. We hope this guide will not only make your life easier but will also help you prepare your team so they can better hear and respond to God's voice, and rejoice to be God's instruments of mercy, hope and love.

Our deep desire is that you grow in Christ as you discover the "new thing" that God is doing in the world and let go of those attitudes, assumptions and pre-conceived ideas that are hurtful rather than helpful. May you experience joy as you participate in God's mission to restore relationships in every direction – inward, upward and outward, including with creation.

Responding to God's Call

Make it Fit your Unique Team

Meet the Team where they are at and trust that the Holy Spirit will guide you every step of the way

Use this guide creatively – feel free to adapt it to your team given the members' availability, geographic location and other issues. Some options include:

- **Training on 3 Days:** Ideally, your STM Team Essentials will meet 3 times before the trip (for example, on 3 Saturdays). The first training should be between 4 and 6 months before the trip.

- **On-line training + 1 weekend retreat:** If your team members come from several different churches, you may want to do some preparation "on line" and then meet at least once in person just a few weeks before the trip to work on teambuilding and plan your ministries (perhaps on a Saturday or Sunday afternoon).

- **Training during regular meetings:** Alternatively, if you are working with a youth group or a team of university students, you could conduct the training during your regularly scheduled meetings.

- **Training at the airport.** If you are working with a team whose members come from multiple states, you may want to suggest the team arrange their flight itineraries to meet at a connecting airport, with enough lay over time to do basic team training before arriving in the host country.

- **Training in country (*this is the least desirable option*).** If there is no other option, set aside the first day in the host country to complete the STM Essentials training sessions.

Teams that invest time with one another in Bible study, team building and cross-cultural training get much more out of the experience. They are also much more effective in the host country, and will be better equipped to respond to schedule changes in a healthy way. Remember: God is working on you long before you get on the plane! God is already in the host country.

Additional Reading and Resources

- *Helping Without Hurting in Short Term Missions* by Steve Corbett, Brian Fikkert, Katie Casselberry, 2014

- *Round Trip Participant's Guide: for use with Documentary and Curriculum* by Chris Blumhofer and Andy Crouch, Christianity Today International, 2008.

- *Walking with the Poor: Principles and Practices of Transformational Development* by Bryant Meyers, 2011

- Use Prayer of Saint Francis as devotional guide while in country

- *Marginalized, Maligned & Miraculous Women in Scripture* by Deborah Spink Winters, 2019 (for small group study)

- *The Friendship of Women: The Hidden Tradition of the Bible* by Joan Chittister, 2006 (for small group study)

- *Just Walk Across the Room: Simple Steps Pointing People to Faith* by Bill Hybels, 2006 (for post-trip debriefing)

Identify Your Team Leader(s)

Some teams have one leader who is responsible for the overall organization of the trip. Other teams have two or more leaders who take responsibility for different aspects of the trip.

- **Team Leader**: Responsible for the overall organization of the trip including destination, coordination with the on-site global servant or partner, project, timeframe, and team member recruitment.

- **Logistics Coordinator**: Research and coordinate important administrative details such as flights, visas, COVID-19 protocol, housing, project supplies, etc.

- **Devotional and Reflection Coordinator**: Facilitate the training sessions before you leave and devotional/reflection times once you're in the host country.

Research basic information about your STM experience at least 12 months before your trip. Use this checklist to keep track of your notes.

1. Contact the Short-Term Mission team at International Ministries: volunteers@internationalministries.org or 1-610-768-2168 to get initial information on items listed below. Then contact the host country global servant* or partners to discuss these items:

    a. Purpose of the trip (Discovery or Learning trip? Construction? Teaching?)

    _____

    b. Possible dates (local weather, seasonal illness, local holidays and festivals)

    _____

    c. Maximum/minimum group size/age limitations _____

    d. Costs for transportation (flights & luggage allowances and fees)

    _____

    e. Costs for lodging, food** (see note below)

    _____

    f. How and whether to send money to the country in advance

    _____

    g. Equipment & Supply needs

    _____

    h. Country contact person(s) (name, position, e-mail, phone, fax)

    _____

    i. Leadership from the organization on site

    _____

    j. Medical facilities

    _____

    k. Safety and security concerns

    _____

    i. COVID-19 Protocol

    _____

* **Coordinating with your IM global servant**: The more input you have from your host global servants and national partners from the start, the more effective your training sessions will be. Make the effort to learn as much as you can before you arrive in the host country. The first step in your preparation is to research your global servant's ministry and host country context on the International Ministries web site: http://internationalministries. org Please be sensitive regarding the number of emails you send to your global servant asking for information.

** **Cost fluctuation**: Allow at least a 10% increase in costs due to currency fluctuations in the 4 to 6 months before your trip. For example, in January, the dollar may be worth 3 pesos. By July, it may be worth only 2.17 pesos.

2. Contact a travel agent regarding travel arrangements. Please contact International Ministries for information on travel agencies experienced in working with short-term mission teams.

    a. Flight costs_____

    b. Flight times and routes _____

    c. Luggage allowances and fees _____

    d. Travel insurance cost_____

3. Develop an estimated budget covering transportation (air & land), food, lodging, project and STM registration fee plus additional cost if an IM staff accompanies you on the trip. See the STM Budget Estimate form at the end of this section.

4. Research visas and medical requirements for the country.

    a. Visa requirements: https://travel.state.gov/content/travel/en/international-travel.html

    b. Medical information on country and vaccines needed/required: http://wwwnc.cdc.gov/travel/

5. Familiarize yourself with the seven STM Standards of Excellence – see https://soe.org/7-standards/ or click here for a PDF of the booklet: https://soe.org/wp-content/uploads/SOE_Booklet.pdf

6. Familiarize yourself with the online STM registration process on this web site: https://portal.internationalministries.org/global-service-opportunities

7. If your whole team comes from one church, you may want to use part of a session to help team members complete the STM online registration process. If team members come from more than one church, you may ask STM staff at International Ministries to help with the online registration process.

STM BUDGET ESTIMATE

TEAM COSTS (PER PERSON):

1. Airfare   _____

2. Travel Insurance   _____

3. In-country transportation   _____

4. Food & Lodging   _____

5. Project Supplies   _____

6. STM Registration Fee   _____

7. IM Administration Fee   _____

TOTAL per person   _____

This is the amount the person will pay "up front."

PERSONAL COSTS

1. Passport, Visa   _____

2. Immunizations   _____

3. Food in transit   _____

4. Gifts for hosts   _____

5. Souvenirs   _____

6. Incidentals   _____

TOTAL per person _____

This is the amount each team member will need for other expenses.

Session One Guide —
4 to 6 months before departure (2.5 – 3 hour session)

Together on the Journey

QUICK LOOK

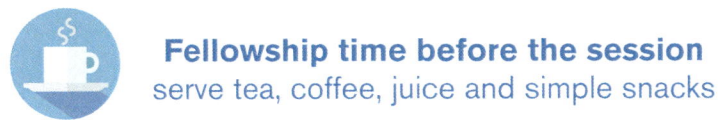

INTRODUCTIONS

20 min

1. Welcome – Introduce team leader(s) and their experience with STM trips.

2. Team introductions
   Invite people to form pairs. Ask your partner:

   - Have you ever gone to **another country** and if so, what did you learn from the experience?

   - **Why do you feel called** to this short-term mission (STM) trip?

   - What is one common **food** and one strange food you would have trouble eating? Then have each person introduce their partner.

3. Pray for the team's conversations, relationships, and preparations.

WHERE AND WHEN ARE WE GOING?

15 min

1. Country and global servant or host country partner _____
   (If you have prayer cards for the global servant, make sure to have them available).

2. Have someone find the destination city on a map (paper or online).

3. Global Servant or host country information – describe the ministry and context of the people with whom the team will work.

4. Dates of our trip _____

5. General schedule: Arrive on _____. Spend the first day in _____, then on to _____ . Fly home on _____.

6. We have been invited to _____ (learn about the Christian community in the host country, coordinate a VBS, help build a parsonage, visit a ministry with street kids, be part of hospitality events, facilitate English conversation groups, etc.)

7. Hand out a **Trip Info Sheet** that includes: host country and global servant contact, dates, purpose, costs (including deposit required), team leader(s) and email/cell number, team leader email/cell number, and group session dates.

1. We are going "Together with God" on this journey.

   Divide the team into 3 groups and assign one passage to each group.

   a. Gen. 12:1-3

   b. Ps. 139:1-10

   c. Matt. 28:18-20

   Ask the small groups to present their responses to these questions:

   - What do these passages tell us about God's role in our mission trip?

   - About our individual and corporate role in God's mission?

     [Possible responses:

     - Mission is God's idea.

     - This is God's mission; God has invited us to be part of it.

     - God will be with us wherever we go, even to the other side of the ocean/globe.

     - Jesus sends us to reach all kinds of people in all kinds of places/countries, all people groups and tribes.

     - Jesus will be with us.]

2. Together with one another.

   Read Eph. 4:1-6

   Considering this passage, how should our team members relate to one another?

   [Maintain our oneness in Christ through humility, gentleness, patience, love, peace and worthy living.]

   > "Be devoted to one another in love. Honor one another above yourselves."
   >
   > Rom. 12:10

3. Together with our in-country hosts.

   Read Rom. 12:10; Heb. 13:1.

   In small groups, memorize Rom. 12:10 *Be devoted to one another in love. Honor one another above yourselves.*

   How should we interact with our in-country hosts according to these two verses?

   [Do no harm while trying to help. Show respect to our hosts. Work together with them since we are part of the same family of God.]

These four questions spell out "**GOD'S**" principles for healthy STM teams.

1. **G**: God's mission. Describe the purpose of our Team. The big picture [cooperate with God in God's mission – see above]. Discover what God is doing in_____ (country/city) and find ways to cooperate.

2. **O**: Open heart, open hands. Observe, ask why, listen. Adopt the attitude of a learner. Prioritize the Majority World Church perspective on STM teams – learn to see through the eyes of our hosts.

3. **D**: Doing is less important than being. What is our "job" as a team?
How can we maintain a healthy balance between building relationships and building a school or church?

   - What advice might Jesus give our team?

4. **S**: a Servant's heart. What should our attitude be as we interact with our hosts and one another?
A servant heart is the foundation of our ministry. Read John 13:12 – 15.

   - What would this look like on our trip?
   What would it NOT look like?

WHY ARE WE GOING? ARE WE TOURISTS OR SERVANTS? WHAT ARE WE GOING TO DO? OR NOT DO?

20 min

WHO ARE WE?

25 min

1. Who are we? In pairs, ask each other:

   - What do you enjoy doing? (e.g. your job, studies, hobbies, fun activities)

   - What kinds of things do other people often ask you to do?

   - Why do you think God has invited you to be on this team?

> *Open the eyes of my heart, Lord I want to see You...*

Draw a large circle (15 cm) in the middle of a flip chart paper. Ask someone to write names of team members and their skills/interests around the circle.

   - As a group: What are some words that describe us as a team?

   Write these in the circle in the middle, in a different color.

   Post on the wall.

2. Team Sit - Stand in a circle facing inward, shoulders touching. Have

everyone turn 90 degrees to the right and put their hands on the shoulders of the person in front of them. Ask everyone to take one "baby step" toward the center of the circle. Then, on the count of three, everyone should carefully sit down together – on the lap of the person behind them.

This works with almost all sizes of people if everyone sits down together. However, if one or more people hesitate or sit too soon, the whole team will end up on the floor laughing.

What does this illustrate about working as a team?

◆ Costs: Estimated total = $_____/person

- $____ round trip fare (your city to destination)

- $____ food, housing, and transportation. Briefly describe housing situation. For example: we'll stay at an inexpensive hotel; or, our team will divide up and stay with host families

- $____ vaccinations – Hep A, Typhoid, others? https://wwwnc.cdc.gov/travel/

- $____ other expenses (gifts for hosts? Unexpected costs, etc.)

- $____ Registration fee & process with STM

IMPORTANT: Start the registration process ASAP; ask each member to complete the new online registration process on the IM website: https://portal.internationalministries.org/global-service-opportunities

Send $____ deposit to _____ (church, regional office) by _____ (date). We need to buy tickets when the price is still low.

◆ Fundraising and Prayer Partners

1. Team prayer partners and fundraising

- We are sent by our church family – not just by ourselves.

- We need to invite people (church members, family, friends) to participate in this ministry through prayer, preparation of materials, and financial support.

- People want to bless your hands and feet and mouth. Share what God is calling you to do.

- Brainstorm fundraising ideas: themed dinner, sell products we've made (art, baked goods, etc.), car wash, sell services (lawn mowing, cook a dinner, babysit, etc.)

✅ Denotes task that needs to be done

✅ Who would like to coordinate our team fundraising? The whole team is responsible for fundraising. This person will serve as the coordinator.

An interesting idea: Ask supporters to sponsor the team costs for one day.

2. Individual fundraising

- Invite friends and family members to participate in this ministry by giving money and praying for you. Encourage each team member to select at least one prayer partner.

- Share a sample fundraising letter.

3. Web sites with fundraising ideas:

- https://blog.fundly.com/fundraising-ideas/

- https://www.eventbrite.com/blog/fundraising-ideas-ds00/

PASSPORTS, VISAS, MEDICAL, BACKGROUND CHECK

20 min

To save time, send this information to team members BEFORE the session. Use this time to review the requirements and respond to questions.

1. Review travel advice from US Travel web site for the host country: https://travel.state.gov/content/travel/en/international-travel.html

2. PASSPORT: ✅ must be valid until at least 6 months after the return date.

3. VISA information: apply online? Receive on arrival? Tourist visas are generally valid for 30 days.

4. REGISTRATION with International Ministries:

✅ Each team member must register through the new online registration process https://portal.internationalministries.org/global-service-opportunities

5. MEDICAL:

✅ Check on vaccinations needed for _____. Example: MMR, DtP, varicella (chickenpox), polio, flu shot. Good idea: Hep A, Typhoid. Malaria. See: https://wwwnc.cdc.gov/travel Team members should consult with their physician regarding immunizations, COVID related protocol and health issues.

All group members must complete the Volunteer Medical Release/Emergency Contact Form (Construction work only) or the Volunteer Medical Release/Emergency Contact Form (Non-Construction work only) on the Resources for Short-Term Mission page https://www.internationalministries.org/resources-for-short-term-mission/.

If you have questions about any of these requirements or documents, please contact IM at volunteers@internationalministries.org

6. Travel Accident Insurance

Once registered with IM, each team member will be covered by supplemental Travel Accident Insurance from AIG Life Insurance Company. The Travel Accident Insurance policy provides:

- $50,000 Medical Evacuation coverage

- $25,000 Accidental Death and Dismemberment coverage

- $10,000 Repatriation of mortal remains

- $5,000 Accident-related medical treatment

- Additional benefits: Medical and legal assistance

7. Your team will also be added to the IM Prayer Network.

8. BACKGROUND CHECK:

✅ Each adult team member must complete an online background check. Please go to the following link: https://www. internationalministries.org/resources-for-short-term-mission/ to complete the Background Check Application form. Click on "Proceed". Have your driver's license and your passport handy, as you will need this information. The secure online application will time out at 40 minutes. If your church has processed a background check on your behalf within the last two years, we will accept those results.

OUR NEXT GATHERINGS
5 min

- STM Team gathering #2 _____ (date)

- STM Team gathering #3 _____ (date)

Assignment – read the article "**Some thoughts about short mission trips**" and post a comment on our WhatsApp group or Facebook group page.

CLOSING PRAYER
5 min

Prayer time – who and what should we pray for?

- team members and leaders,

- the host country team,

- that God would use us to demonstrate his love.

Close in prayer

Photo by Daniel Buttry

TRIP INFO SHEET

Where exactly are we going? (country, name and location of ministry)

_____

e.g. The Dios Con Nosotros Seminary, Mexicali, Mexico

When? Dates   _____

What we hope to do: _____

Describe the purpose of the trip. Example: Discover how God is working through the believers in Mexico. We will help construct a new classroom at the seminary. We will also serve alongside the local church members in their VBS ministry or food delivery and visitation ministry.

How much will it cost? _____

Include a payment schedule. The first deposit should cover the plane ticket by time of reservation/purchase at three to four months before the trip. Include a note that the price of the trip is subject to change due to inflation or other reasons. Also factor the cost of airline travel insurance to cover date changes once travel has started and other emergencies. And any extra lodging days due to COVID-19 quarantine restrictions.

Who is in charge and how to contact them:

_____

Team Leader(s) name, email, cell phone number

Team training session dates: _____

Team members are expected to participate in all 3 team training sessions.

FUNDRAISING SAMPLE LETTER

Dear _____,

I need your help as I step out in faith for the Lord. This spring break/summer I will be part of a short-term mission team from our church/region that is going to _____ _____ (country and dates)

Our main goal as a team is to   _____.

While we are in _____, we will be

_____

(describe your project or the nature of your trip).

I am really excited to see what God will teach me and to see how God will use me, too! (Insert a photo or a map of the country here)

I would really appreciate your prayers for: _____

It would be awesome if you could help support our team financially. Each person on our team needs to raise $ _____. I have already raised $ _____ but still need to raise $ _____ before _____ (date).

If you are able, please donate $25, $50 or whatever you feel led to give toward our support. Please go to our church web site here and make your tax-deductible gift. Note in the reference that it is a gift for the mission trip to (country name) with fundraising credit to [your name].

Thank you. Your prayer and financial support mean a lot to our team.

Love In Christ,

(Your name)

AECB, SD July 2020

SOME THOUGHTS ABOUT SHORT MISSION TRIPS

In his book *Toxic Charity*, Robert Lupton writes, contrary to popular belief, most missions trips don't empower those being served, engender healthy cross-cultural relationships, improve quality of life, relieve poverty, change the lives of participants or increase support for long-term missions work. He says in the short time that's available projects can easily become more important than people. Here are some ways to do a short-term missions trip well:

Encourage the worker, rather than "the children."

The most effective form of short-term ministry is to encourage the local missionaries and their national staff, rather than beneficiaries. In fact **some places have rules in place to protect vulnerable children from attachment and abandonment issues that having short term visitors can bring**. You may not be able to impact those kids in the short time you are there, but you can impact the local staff. Encouragement can go a long way. Most local workers have lots of good ideas that rarely ever turn out as planned. They are the people who are there every day loving people and doing the hard stuff. They spend countless hours in uncomfortable situations. You don't live there so you might not get it, but be a 'safe place' for them to air things out without judgment or reproach. Offer grace and encouragement; develop a connection that will remain long after you leave. You might be the lifeline of support they need and you might learn a lot from them in the process.

Handouts? — don't!

If you roll in and hand out a bunch of soccer balls and candy to kids, it undermines the bridges of trust local workers have built through partnering and instead sends the message of easy "Aid" and spreads dependency. If you have gifts, only bring what the local worker has asked

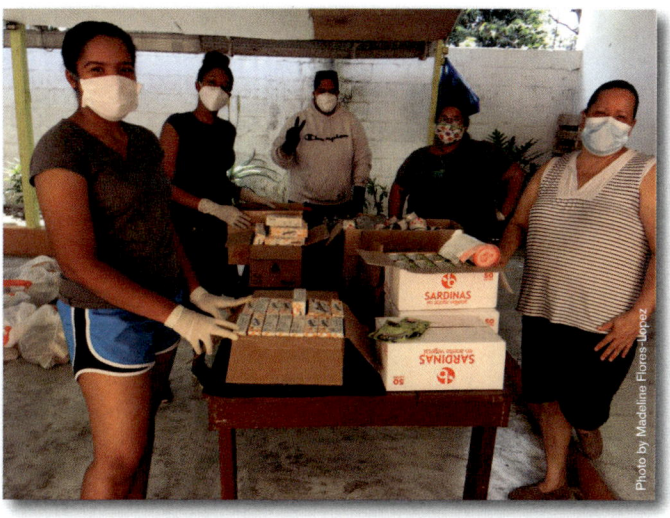

for and let them hand it out at a time they deem appropriate. Ask what their needs are. It's better to fit into something they are already doing than create a new routine or program. Don't give money to anyone other than the organization or global servant you have built a trusted relationship with who has an accountability system in place; let them distribute the funds to the areas of most need. If you don't have a trusted relationship with accountability, then do not give money.

The issue of imbalances of power due to wealth/poverty is serious. In very little time you can create un-healthy patterns of dependency or even resentment. You can do more harm to the local ministry than good. This ranges from the 'saviour' complex that places everyone else as a victim to be rescued, to the belittling of leaders in developing nations, to the handing out of gifts and cash because of guilt and the desire to feel good about one's self. I've seen well-meaning people destroy locals with handouts. I've also seen good hearted Westerners get taken for a ride, only to lose a lot of money on an "orphanage" that was never built. **Be generous with your time and talents instead.**

Test your motives

Let God purify the motives of your heart. Is it for approval, or a pat on the back? To prove your worth to the world and yourself? Is it so you can have some cute kids from another country on your Facebook feed? Don't think about all the cool stories or photos you want to bring back so you can show people what you've done. Ask God to reveal to you why He wants you there. Think about committing to that place or group of people in some way in the future.

Be a learner, be relational

You're not going to solve world poverty in the few days you have on the ground, nor should you try. Don't go with answers but go searching for answers — and recognize there might not be any simple ones. Learning the context of a country takes time. Trust the locals' perspective. You might just sit and listen to someone's story. That also involves being vulnerable. This is messy, challenging, work, but if you look close enough you just might find some grace and hope trickling through the resilience of the people.

Respect cultural and social norms

Try to understand the why behind how the culture is, versus judging it. Learn a few words of their local language. Build relationships by not offending people. Follow the rules of your hosts even if you don't understand them. Don't look down on people as "less educated." Remember the missionaries and locals are experts on their own place. Please respect the national staff and follow their recommendations.

Be flexible

It's going to be tough; many things may not go according to schedule or plan, and huffing and puffing isn't going to change anything. Most other cultures move a lot slower than the West and they are not on your time-table. Your agenda may not happen. See what God's agenda is. Anything can be endured for a short time. Take a breather, if you need to. Get some personal time or discuss being outside of your comfort zone with someone.

Be compassionate and kind, but don't be led by needs. Be led by the Holy Spirit.

It is not your responsibility or even the local workers' responsibility to meet all the needs of every single person. Jesus didn't meet every need and we shouldn't try to either. Effective ministries have a vision and a clear focus and they stick to it. Your emotions will be stirred up but try to decipher between your heart strings and God's actual voice and be obedient. Use wisdom. When in doubt, check with your team leader to see what is appropriate. Don't tell a kid you're going to "sponsor" them. Don't make promises you can't keep and don't put the local workers in the position to clean up your mess.

Remember that success is not defined by numbers, or even outcomes, but by whether or not you've been obedient to what God asked you to do.

Follow through

Think about how you can make this trip actually change your life. Think about things that would be helpful for you to do once you return home. **Your biggest impact may very well be after you leave.**

(Notes adapted from '10 Steps for Doing Short Term Missions Trips Well' by Sarita Hartz, May 2017.)

Session Two Guide —
4 to 6 weeks before departure
(2.5 – 3 hour session)

Cross-Cultural Relationship Building

QUICK LOOK

Fellowship time before the session
serve tea, coffee, juice and simple snacks
(if they can be from the country you will be serving in, even
better. If not, be creative with what you serve. Consider fair
trade items & serving without using any paper goods.)

CHECK IN ON PROGRESS
10 min

1. Check in: How have you experienced God's blessing in these areas? Do you need any help?

   a. Fundraising progress – be sure to send thank you notes or texts to those who pledge or give.

   b. Passports and medical prep

2. Review the memory verse from Session 1: *Be devoted to one another in love. Honor one another above yourselves.* Rom. 12:10

3. Praise God for walking with us on this journey; pray that God would continue to guide our steps.

> "Be devoted to one another in love. Honor one another above yourselves."
>
> Rom. 12:10

GETTING TO KNOW OUR HOST COUNTRY
40 min

1. Learning the language – survival phrases

   - Invite someone who speaks the language of the host country to come and teach the group basic survival phrases. (Hello, what is your name, my name is _____, yes, no, please, thank you, where is the toilet, etc.). Consider inviting an international university student. Or use a You Tube video if no one is available.

   - In pairs, practice the words and phrases with each other.

   - Pass around a bowl of M&Ms to practice, "please, thank you, yes, no, what is your name, my name is".

   - Distribute a **Survival Phrases** sheet to the team via email or social media.

2. Host country basic information
   Present a PowerPoint highlighting (prepare this beforehand):

   - Location of the country and its neighboring country (ies)

   - People and places where you will be going

   - Basic demographic info – e.g. population, religion, political structure

   - Typical foods

   - Typical dress

   - Customs and courtesy – how to greet someone properly, cultural Do's and Don'ts

3. Learn a short praise song in the host country language – the team will very likely sing this song in different contexts on the trip. Ask your hosts (global servants or host country partners) to suggest a simple praise song if you are not sure.

4. Host partner overview: history, ministries, how the team might be a blessing to the partners.

   ▪ Name and ministry focus of the global servant or partner organization. Research the ministry of the global servant you will visit – see the International Ministries ABCUSA web site to locate the global servant(s) who will be your primary host(s): https://www.internationalministries.org/

   ▪ Find pertinent facts about the global servant(s); such as years of service in that area? What are their ministry areas? Do they have children?

   ▪ If you are visiting a church or Baptist Association or faith-based organization: When was it founded? By whom? What was their purpose? What does the organization do now? Who benefits from the ministry?

CROSS-CULTURAL RELATIONSHIP BUILDING

30 min

Am I willing to be uncomfortable outside my comfort zone and be stretched in Jesus' name?

1. Challenging stereotypes

We often carry with us stereotypes about the people and culture of other countries. How might this affect our relationships with our hosts?

Watch this video together. It is produced by a group of students and academics of a Norwegian development agency to challenge perceptions about poverty and development.

▪ What is funny about this video? What is sad?

   Video: *Africa for Norway* - charity single. https://www.youtube.com/watch?v=oJLqyuxm96k&list=RDpkOUCvzqb9o&index=5

▪ Discuss the funny and sad elements of the video.

Watch the next video that responds to the message of the first video. *Why Africans don't need to help the freezing Norwegians.* https://www.youtube.com/watch?v=9JmdK0fA34s&list=RDpkOUCvzqb9o&index=1

▪ What lessons could we learn from these videos and apply to our STM trip?

- What attitudes/behaviors (US stereotypes) we need to tone down when we travel abroad?

Write them down on a whiteboard or paper and distribute them to the team. Alternatively, invite everyone to take a photo of the list, or post it in your social media group.

2. Building healthy cross-cultural relationships

Remember "Open heart, open hands" from GODS principles for successful mission trips from our first session? (Ps. 18:27) The best way to approach another culture is with the attitude of a respectful, humble learner. Below is a practical strategy for interacting in an unfamiliar cultural setting.

3. Observe, Ask, Listen (**OAL**)

And take delight in noticing commonalities & differences

- **O**bserve – take note of what is happening around you, suspend judgement, note facial expressions and body language. Avoid asking questions at this point – just OBSERVE.

- **A**sk – ask your hosts to help you learn about their culture. You could say, "I noticed that _____ [e.g. everyone takes off their shoes when entering the church.] This is different than in my culture. What does it mean when a person does that?"

  The "I" statement acknowledges that you are a learner and conveys respect for your hosts.

- **L**isten - pay attention to the explanation. Ask for clarification: "Do you mean _____?" Follow up with: "What should I do in this situation to show respect or gratitude?" Asking for guidance conveys a deep sense of humility.

4. If there is time, role play some typical encounters. For example, greeting people, entering a home, sitting on the floor or at a table, with utensils or without, eating unfamiliar food, participating in a meeting, arriving late to a meeting, starting conversations.

The culture shock cycle — this too shall pass.

1. Everything will be quite different when we arrive in the host country — the weather, people, language, smells, dress code, amenities, signs, driving habits, etc. The OAL (Observe, Ask, Listen) strategy will help us to deal with differences in a healthy way with an open heart and mind.

However, there may be times when you feel overwhelmed with all the 'new stuff'. Is this normal? Yep. Almost everyone goes through predictable stages of culture shock when they enter a new culture.

Invite someone to tell a story about their experience with culture shock and how they managed it. Invite a new immigrant from your local community to share their story and culture shock upon arriving in the US.

2. Show the **Stages of Culture Shock** handout and graph (below) and discuss each stage. Each person may go through them at a different pace or intensity, but they still react in similar ways.

- Discuss: How can we support one another when a teammate is experiencing culture shock? [give the teammate a chance to vent his or her feelings in a safe, private way; pray with the person; remind him or her that everyone goes through culture shock; reaffirm your trust in God who called you to this STM experience]

STAGES of CULTURE SHOCK

Honeymoon   *Acceptance*

EMOTIONAL STATE

Adjustment

Anxiety

MONTHS IN NEW COUNTRY

- If the group is larger than 6, share in pairs your culture shock experiences and then invite a couple of people to share what they learned with the larger group.

3. How can we help each other deal with stress? (Phil. 4:6-8, Luke 8:22-25)

Stress is a common, normal response to experiencing new, unfamiliar places, people, food and customs. How can we as individuals and a team respond to stress in a healthy way?

In groups of 3 or 4, share

a) how you can tell that I am stressed,

b) how I have learned to cope with stress, and

c) how you can help me when I am feeling stressed.

Team member roles

1. Brainstorm the tasks or projects related to the trip. Possible activities and ministry opportunities in (name of country) might include:

   ▪ Prayer walks

   ▪ Mission exposure/learning

   ▪ Ministry of presence

   ▪ Art or handicraft projects

   ▪ Music – playing/singing with church praise and worship team

   ▪ Church on Sunday – preach, lead a devotional, participate

   ▪ ESL classes

   ▪ Village visit

   ▪ Visit temples or shrines – learn about the major religion of the host country and spirituality in that context

   ▪ VBS

   ▪ Construction project

   ▪ Youth sports outreach

   ▪ Medical services – general medical care, eye exams

   ▪ Supporting practical needs of global servants (filing, packing, sorting, etc.)

   What are some other team roles that might be important? E.g. take photos and videos of the experience, provide first-aid, lead team devotional and reflection times, etc. See the list of possible **Team Member Roles** at the end of this session.

2. Invite team members to volunteer to coordinate each task or project based on their skills and interests. This gives each member a sense of ownership in the team and lightens your load as a leader. Clarify what each person is expected to do and agree on a timetable. Assure them that you and the whole team will support them as they carry out their responsibility.

   ▪ Ask each of the project coordinators to sketch out their plan, who will work with them, resources needed, and a timeline for preparing the resources if necessary. Remember that we will work together with our hosts to plan projects. Therefore, come up with possible ideas, not a plan carved in stone.

   ▪ Ask each coordinator to set a time to meet with their project team to discuss ideas and pray for the project and the host country partners.

✅ Denotes task that needs to be done

✅ 1. Check that everyone has completed the online registration with STM

✅ 2. Collect the **IM Medical Clearance Form** from each team member to include in your Emergency Plan folder. Each team member needs to upload their form to the online platform at IM or email it to volunteers@internationalministries.org.

3. **Individual Medical Insurance**: The supplemental accident insurance offered by IM does not include coverage of medical treatment for sickness. Each participant should have their own medical insurance that will cover them while out of the country.

4. **Travel authorization for minors**: If you have team members who are under 18, they must have a parental release form signed and notarized if only one or neither of their parents will be going on the mission trip. Team members under 18 should submit their completed **Minor Travel Authorization** form by next week _____ (date).

✅ Note: Keep one copy of the Travel Authorization form in the Emergency Plan folder (see below). Scan and send a copy to volunteers@internationalministries.org.

✅ 5. **EMERGENCY CONTACT PACKET**: Prepare an emergency contact packet that includes;

- A copy of the **Medical Release** form for each team member.

- Names and cell phone numbers for global servant and host country leaders, including the country telephone access codes.

- Detailed itinerary including hotel or guest house addresses and phone numbers.

- Copies of the photo page of each passport.

- A note about the time difference between your home and the time zone of the host country.

- The US State Department number for Emergency Assistance to American Citizens Abroad: +1-202-501-4444

Share this information with the local contact person(s), the team leaders, your pastor and your church office.

- Praise God that God is already in the place you are going. Thank God for bringing you together and providing all you need as a team.

- Pray that God would use your team to encourage the sisters and brothers in Christ in the host country.

- Ask God to guide you in all your plans and preparations.

Cross-cultural evening: Go to an ethnic food restaurant together

Take the team to a restaurant that serves food similar to your host country. Have fun and taste unfamiliar food if possible. Practice reacting to new tastes with grace and humour.

Discuss **The Intimacy of the Table** by H. Nouwen.

Photo by fauxels from Pexels

HANDOUTS PDFS

1. **Survival phrases**
2. **Stages of Culture Shock**
3. **Team Member Roles – some ideas**
4. **Basic First-Aid Kit**
5. **The Intimacy of the Table**

SURVIVAL PHRASES

Greetings

Hello _____

Good morning/afternoon/evening/night

_____

How are you? How are you doing?

_____

I'm fine, thank you

_____

How is your family? What's your name?

_____

My name is _____

God bless you. _____

Courtesy

Please

_____

Thank you

_____

Excuse me

_____

Sorry

_____

Conversation

I (don't) understand.

_____

Please speak slowly.

_____

What does xx mean?

_____

Essentials

Where is the _____ (bathroom)?

_____

I'm thirsty/hungry.

_____

Yes _____ No _____

Numbers

One _____

Two _____

Three _____

Four _____

Five _____

Six _____

Seven _____

Eight _____

Nine _____

Ten _____

STAGES of CULTURE SHOCK

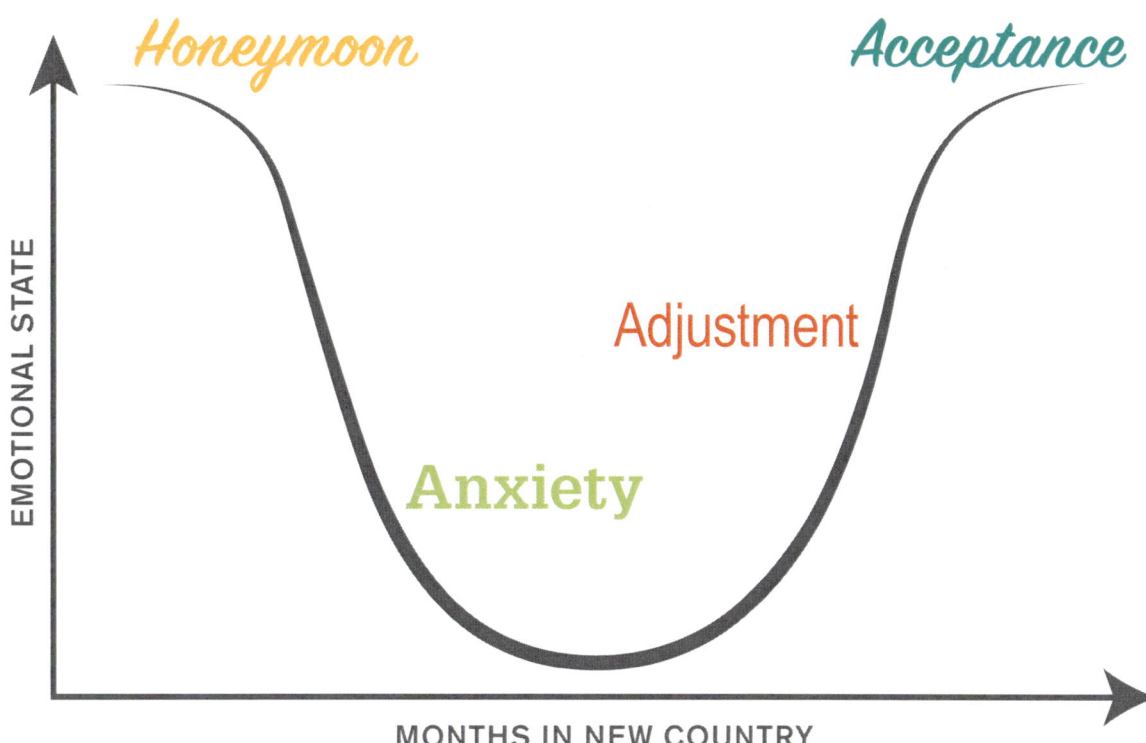

TEAM MEMBER ROLES – SOME IDEAS

Construction Coordinator – works with host coordinator to plan out all construction activities.

Cook – prepares team meals with the assistance of team members.

Cyber Geek – sets up regular communication with home church via e-mail, blog, etc.

Devotional Coordinator – coordinates the daily team devotional times using the Part 2 of this tool kit as a resource: *Watch for God at Work! An in-country Devotional Guide for engaging in God's mission.* This person encourages each team member to sign up to lead a devotion or end of the day reflection moment.

Emergency Coordinator – someone who can keep cool in tense situations (accident, political turmoil, natural disaster) and help the team manage the crisis. This person should also have access to the Emergency Contact file containing the forms for each member.

> We are together on the journey

Gift Coordinator – makes a list of all the gifts brought by team members and coordinates with team leader and hosts regarding the who, when and how of giving.

Keeper of the Online or paper Journal/Blog – asks team members to take turns writing about team activities and impressions in the team journal (e.g. one person may write for the team each day); if in paper form, distributes copies of the journal to all team members upon return home.

Luggage Counter – counts all luggage every time the team is ready to travel. It is helpful to have a count for suitcases and another count for carry-ons and to carry an extra supply of brightly colored yarn for suitcases.

Medic – puts together and carries a team first-aid kit (see **Basic First Aid Kit list**). Make sure the Medic is aware of any special medical needs of team members. Ideally this person should have basic first aid and CPR training.

Music Leader – song leader, piano or guitar player that can lead Praise and Worship and help the team prepare selections to sing at local churches.

People Counter – counts the team members to make sure nobody is left behind!

Photographer – takes photos on behalf of team so that 15 people don't all crowd around the child on the street to get a picture; distributes digital or printed copies of pictures to all team members upon return to the States. See **Photos and Video tips** at the end of session #3.

Reflection Leader – this is probably the team leader; the person who helps the team debrief and reflect on their experiences using Part 2 of this tool kit as a resource: *Watch for God at Work! An in-country Devotional Guide for engaging in God's mission.*

Tailor – brings sewing kit including safety pins.

Team Schedule Coordinator – informs the team about the next day's schedule (in coordination with the team leader), makes sure the team is ready to go on time.

Thank-You-Note Person – keeps track of names and addresses of all hosts, churches, host families, etc. and asks team members to write the thank you notes; uses team monies for stationery and postage. Bring a pack of blank thank you note cards and write some while in country.

Translator – someone fluent (or at least somewhat knowledgeable!) in the local language who can translate for the team. See **Speaking Through an Interpreter** at the end of session #3.

Treasurer – carries team monies, keeps track of all expenses, saves ALL receipts, and prepares the financial report.

VBS Coordinator – works with local coordinator to plan and assign responsibilities for VBS or other educational ministry.

BASIC FIRST-AID KIT

Pack these items in a large zip-lock bag or two to reduce the bulk.

- Aspirin or Tylenol

- Decongestant for colds & flu, e.g. Sudafed/pseudoephedrine
  (take before flights to avoid damaging ears)

- Antihistamine (e.g. Benadryl)

- Triple-antibiotic ointment or germicidal soap

- Band-Aids

- Anti-itch ointment for stings, bites, sunburn (e.g. calamine lotion)

- Diarrhea medication (e.g. Imodium)

- Sunscreen

- Rehydration mixture (in case of severe diarrhea) – Gatorade powder works well

- Laxative

- Pepto-Bismol – chewable is less messy

- Cold & sore throat medication

- Thermometer – for groups of 10 or more, at least 2 thermometers

- Ace bandage

- Water purification tablets

- Bee sting/snake bite kit

- A couple of syringes and needles? (in case you need injections in a country
  with medical hygiene problems). Ask your doctor for a note explaining why they
  have been prescribed.

A more comprehensive list may be found on the Center for Disease Control website
at https://www.cdc.gov/

NOTE: Some hosts may ask for simple medical treatment provided during a mini
clinic scheduled periodically during your stay. Coordinate this in advance with your
hosts.

THE INTIMACY OF THE TABLE

The table is one of the most intimate places in our lives. It is there that we give ourselves to one another. When we say, "Take some more, let me serve you another plate, let me pour you another glass, don't be shy, enjoy it," we say a lot more than our words express. We invite our friends to become part of our lives.

We want them to be nurtured by the same food and drink that nurture us. We desire communion. That is why a refusal to eat and drink what a host offers is so offensive. It feels like a rejection of an invitation to intimacy.

Strange as it may sound, the table is the place where we want to become food for one another. Every breakfast, lunch, or dinner can become a time of growing communion with one another.

Henri J.M. Nouwen
Bread for the Journey

Photo by fauxels from Pexels

Session Three Guide —
5 to 10 days before departure
(2.5 – 3 hour session)

Love One Another

QUICK LOOK

Fellowship time before the session
serve tea, coffee, juice and simple snacks —
preferably comfort food items

<table>
<tr><td>

CHECK IN ON PROGRESS

15 min

</td><td>

1. Check in time – how have you experienced God's presence as you prepared for this trip? What is your experience with journaling so far?

   - Pray — Thank God for giving the team this opportunity to serve. Ask God to keep team members safe and healthy before and during the trip.

2. Let's continue to support each other as we embark on this trip. In pairs, memorize: *Therefore encourage one another and build each other up, just as in fact you are doing.* 1 Thess. 5:11

3. Review basic language phrases from Session 2. Practice counting from 1 to 5 in the language. Have fun as you practice and stumble on pronunciation.

4. Sing the praise song you learned in Session 2 (in the host country language). All your efforts will enrich the cross-cultural experiences you will have in country.

</td></tr>
<tr><td>

LOVE ONE ANOTHER – RELATIONSHIPS WITH OUR HOSTS AND OUR TEAM

45 min

</td><td>

If you are able to coordinate to have a Zoom, Facetime or Skype video chat with the global servant or host during this session, that will be great. Try to keep the conversation to 20 minutes, given time zone difference.

(25 min) Relating to our hosts with a Servant's Heart (John 13:12 – 15)

1. How can we interact with our hosts in a Christ-like way?

Divide the team into two groups. Pass out **STM Team Case Study 1** to one group and **Case Study 2** to the other group.

   - Ask the groups to read their case study and identify guidelines for relating to our hosts with a servant's heart. Provide flipchart paper and markers.

   - After about 10 minutes, invite the groups to present their guidelines based on the case studies.

   Possible guidelines might include:

</td></tr>
</table>

✅ Denotes task that needs to be done

a. Ask our hosts what are THEIR plans & expectations for the project. Plan projects WITH not FOR our hosts whenever possible. LISTEN before DOING. This is a great time to practice listening skills.

b. Be willing to do things according to our hosts' plan; don't insist on your way. It is a time to shine in humility. Don't assume we know what's best.

c. If we have a suggestion for doing things differently, check it out with our hosts first.

> You never get a second chance to make a first impression. How you say "Hello" matters

d. If there is a safety issue involved in how something is done, discuss this openly with our hosts (e.g. how to wire an electrical outlet, the load bearing capacity of a support beam in the new school building, ratio of children and adults in an activity, etc.)

e. We are going to preach the gospel (in deed and word) not North American culture.

f. Remember that the buildings we build are not as important as the relationships we build! Build relationships to God's code. Be fully present when interacting with our hosts. Doing is less important than being – See GOD'S principles for healthy STM teams from Session One.

✅ Send the list of guidelines to the team.

(20 min) Dealing with conflict

1. Read Matthew 18:15-20. What practical guidelines does Jesus give us for managing conflict?

- Begin by approaching the person one-on-one;

- If that doesn't work, ask one or two others to help mediate the discussion;

- Bring it before the whole team only if the first two steps aren't successful.

What would be the opposite of Jesus' approach?

- Talk to everyone but the person who has offended you

- Try to get people to take your side

- Refuse to forgive the offender even after he or she apologizes

- Let your irritation fester until you are really angry

2. What do Ephesians 4:25-27 and James 1:19-20 teach about how to handle anger and hurt feelings?

- What might be some possible sources of conflict in our team while we are on this mission trip? What are some of our pet peeves?

- How do people usually react to conflict? (e.g. avoid, give in, attack, compromise)

- How do these approaches compare to Jesus' guidelines in Matthew 18 and the other passages we just read?

3. Considering our discussion of these passages, what is our promise to each other on the team about how we will deal with conflict?

- The first step is to pray — ask God to give you grace and wisdom to deal with the conflict in a healthy way that preserves relationships. Take a moment to pray.

- Adapt the guidelines based on Matt. 18 generated in item #1 above.

✅ Send the final list to the team.

TEAM COMMUNICATION

10 min

1. Team blog

- Create a team blog.

- Ask for volunteers to post each day beginning about 3 days before you leave for the host country.

- Include prayer requests and praises.

2. Photos and videos: the subject-object dilemma — How might the camera become a hindrance to building healthy relationships? Don't let the camera be the way to say your first "hello." Note that sometimes people being photographed feel like they are merely 'objects.' Others wonder if the visitors will sell the photos to make money. Always ask permission before taking someone's picture.

What shall we do as a team to demonstrate respect to our hosts when it comes to taking photographs and videos?

- Ask permission to take photos.

- Avoid posting pictures of minors on social media.

- Have one person take photos — not all 12 team members!

- Offer to share photos with our hosts.

3. Create a social media group to share non-emergency public information with family and friends back home (e.g. "we've arrived!", praises and prayer requests, etc.)

4. Invite your sending church to pray for the team and to pray for our hosts.

   - Set up a prayer roster with the prayer partners you have selected, and ask them to lead prayers for the team on a specific day.

   - Ask the church to pray for the team during Sunday morning worship, youth group meetings, prayer team gatherings, and/or send prayer requests via email to church members.

   - Schedule with the pastor a commissioning service of the team on the last Sunday before the team leaves.

PACKING TIPS

10 min

1. **Packing list** –Briefly go over the items on the list. Note the dress code for the host country. Our team is committed to showing respect for our hosts by honoring their cultural dress codes (1 Corinthians 10:23-24). For example, in some countries it is unacceptable for adult men or women to wear shorts in public, even when it is blistering hot. In other countries, everyone removes their shoes before entering a house or house of worship.

2. Packing tips

   - Pack only as much as you yourself can carry over a bumpy road for a mile.

   - Pack ONE suitcase and one carry-on backpack.

   - Pack very little or no jewelry.

GIVING TO DO NO HARM

40 min

1. Let's take a look at two real-life examples of well-intentioned gift giving that had unhappy results. Divide the team into two smaller groups and pass out the '**Giving to do no Harm**' case studies.

2. Ask the small groups to respond to the following questions after they have read their case study:

   - What was good and Christ-like about what happened?

     - giving to help others,

     - generosity,

     - compassionate hearts,

     - wanting to make someone else happy,

     - maybe provide an opening for sharing the Gospel.

- What were some of the not-so-great motivations possibly behind the Americans' giving?

  - giving to reduce my feelings of guilt at having so much

  - "I'm a Christian – I don't have to pay attention to this stingy pastor."

  - "I wouldn't allow my kids to accept candy from a stranger but it's OK to do that here."

- What are some of the unintended effects of the generosity of STM teams?

  - creates dependency,

  - teaches others to be beggars,

  - causes jealousy between those who get something and those who don't.

3. Bring the group back together and ask them why they feel they should give gifts.

   - We need to share what we have; because God tells us to give to others.

   - Because it makes us feel like we are doing something pleasing to God.

   - Because we need to do our part to relieve some suffering in the world.

4. Generate a list of your team's guidelines for giving gifts. How can we give gifts in a truly loving way that does no harm?

   - Check with the host or global servant before giving any gifts.

   - Better yet, have the host give them out during a special occasion even after the team has gone.

   - Give gifts to the local denominational body, school, or orphanage to distribute to the neediest rather than giving directly to individuals.

5. Sometimes, a team wants to take some small gifts to the global servants and their children they will meet. What is appropriate? It is best to ask them what they miss most from home. If that is not possible, here are some suggestions:

   - mixes (bread, cakes, jello, pudding, cheesecake)

- books for the kids

- nuts, candy bars (check with global servants if children have any nut allergies)

- family/group games, puzzles, small board games

6. You may also want to take small gifts to your hosts. Here are some suggestions:

- photos of yourself, your family, your church, your team

- postcards from home

- pens/pencils and paper

- key chains, bookmarks

- a craft from your area

- small puzzles

- hand held stress balls

- coloring books for children and adults

- Scripture calendar

- mugs

- personal soaps

- hygiene kits (washcloth, toothbrush, soap/shampoo, comb)

- towel/washcloth

> **Interesting Linguistic Trivia:**
>
> Americans *"keep"* time
>
> South Africans *"have"* time
>
> Brazilians *"give"* time

Receiving with grace

1. Most Westerners find it very hard to receive from others, especially from people who seem to have so little from a material standpoint. Yet true friendship and partnership means both giving AND receiving. We need to learn to receive with grace and joy.

2. Ask the team to respond to these questions:

- What do you hope to gain from this experience?

- What are you hoping to receive from others?

- How can you express your appreciation without "paying" for such gifts, especially when they are given with great sacrifice?

1. Keeping healthy – Write/print each of the tips in large print on a ½ page sized paper. Distribute them to team members and invite them to post their tip on the wall or whiteboard.

The Center for Disease Control (CDC) web site has health and safety information on every country: https://wwwnc.cdc.gov/travel

Tips from the CDC website:

- Get vaccinated as recommended.

- Follow COVID-19 protocol.

- Take antimalarial meds if recommended.

- Eat and drink safely – drink bottled water, avoid ice unless safe.

- Prevent bug bites – use repellent.

- Wear sunscreen – SPF 30 or higher.

- Reduce your exposure to germs – wash hands regularly with soap and water; eat food that is "straight from the stove"; avoid fresh fruits and veggies (unless you peel them).

- Avoid direct contact with animals.

2. Safety tips

- Go with a buddy. Don't go wandering around alone day or night.

- Let your team leader know where you are going.

- Follow the team leader's and hosts' instructions.

- Stay alert but not paranoid.

- Stay with the crowds and the traffic.

- Don't leave your bags unattended.

- Carry only small amounts of cash (if you carry a "secret stash" somewhere on your body, don't expose the hiding place in public).

- Keep a hand on your bag; carry your wallet in a front pocket.

- Carry your backpack in front of you if at all possible.

IMPORTANT: Each member should carry host and global servant contact information: name, phone number, street address.

1. Distribute the Team Travel Itinerary – housing, meals, transportation plans. See sample **Team Travel Itinerary** at the end of this Session.

   Tell the team what time to meet at the pick-up point or what time and where to meet at the airport. Go through check-in as a group at the airport.

   - You may be able to do a preliminary check-in online the day before, however, for most destinations, you will still need to do a final check-in at the airport so that they can confirm your visa and dispatch your suitcase.

   TIP: Tie brightly colored yarn on each suitcase (one color for the whole team).

2. Tentative daily schedule & devotional schedule – see the **In-Country Devotional and Reflection Guide** for STM Teams. Note that plans almost always change, so the team will need to be flexible and hold the schedule with an "open hand." See the **Sample Daily Schedules** at the end of this Session.

3. Explain how to get currency in the host country – Are there ATMs available? Can you exchange USD for local currency?

1. Post-trip gatherings – set a date to meet with the group within 10 days of your return home.

2. Set a date for the Team to present your experience and thank your sending church and prayer partners.

Pray for one another, the team, your hosts and your supporters.

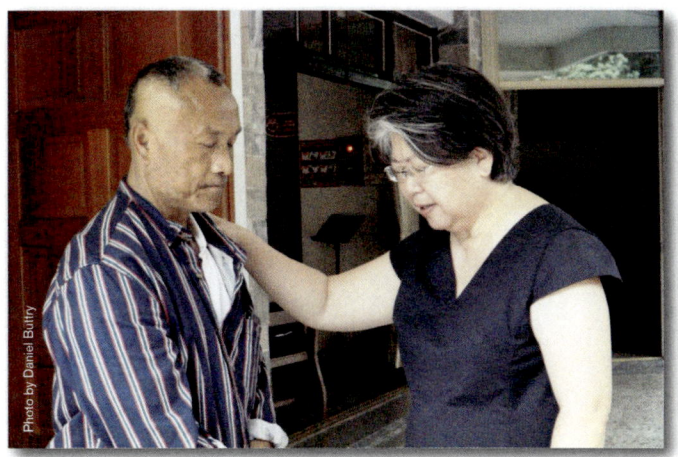

Photo by Daniel Buttry

HANDOUTS PDFS

1. **STM Team Case Study 1**

2. **STM Team Case Study 2**

3. **Giving to Do No Harm – Case Study 1**

4. **Giving to Do No Harm – Case Study 2**

5. **Packing List**

6. **Team Travel Itinerary**

7. **Sample Daily Schedules**

Send to Team members:

1. **Tips for Managing Jet Lag**

2. **Tips for Speaking Through an Interpreter**

3. **Photos and Video tips**

STM CASE STUDY 1

A church from West Virginia decided to serve in Costa Rica for two weeks. From the very beginning, the team was committed to investing significant time to prepare for the trip. They gathered information about the country and then talked directly with International Ministries' partners in Costa Rica.

One of the first questions to the Costa Ricans was, "What do you want us to do?" The church then put together an intergenerational team with the skills needed. They met together regularly before the trip to polish their cross-cultural ministry skills, learn some basic Spanish, and plan the project.

They knew, however, that they would still need to be flexible even with all this advance communication and preparation.

The Costa Rican partners had asked them to construct another classroom for the seminary, so the team rented a cement mixer for the job.

However, just as they began work, the power abruptly went out for a day and a half. Consequently, there was no power for the cement mixer and no lights to work by. This was a huge set back, but the team did not lose heart. They asked their Costa Rican partners for advice. "Should we stop working? Should we shift to another project? What do you recommend that we do?" The answer was simple: the hosts taught the team how to mix cement by hand and the project moved forward!

The team lived with host families during their time in country. They knew it might cramp their style and make them less "efficient," but they felt this was important in order to learn and to develop a personal relationship with their Costa Rican sisters and brothers. Each team member learned a great deal from their hosts about Costa Rican culture, customs, and family structure. The relationships built during this "downtime" turned out to be one of the most valuable parts of the trip!

Another highlight for the team was their daily prayer and reflection time. They gathered for about 15-20 minutes each evening to reflect on their experiences and what God was teaching them. In addition, they met after lunch each day with the Costa Rican project leaders to evaluate the progress of the work.

The Costa Rican hosts later expressed their deep appreciation for the flexibility and servant heart of the team. They felt that the team's spirit of respect and openness overcame the barriers of language and culture. They concluded "Never has it been so exciting to work alongside our brothers and sisters from the North."

From the notes of Jim Wiegner, former missionary serving in Costa Rica.

STM CASE STUDY 2

A team from California arrived on the job site in Haiti ready to work on a building project started several years before. The previous year, three of the twelve members had worked putting up the walls of the second floor of the housing project. This years' goal was to finish the project by pouring the concrete roof. The Haitian project boss had been the boss the previous year and already knew three of the team members. All others were new to the project and unknown to the team.

On the first day, the visiting team eagerly jumped into the work measuring, cutting and nailing the lumber into the needed forms. The Haitian workers quickly faded from the scene and the assumption was that they had gone on a 'coffee break.' However, they did not return for a long time and someone finally noticed that they were gathered on the ground floor in the shade.

When the visiting team went to lunch the Haitian crew returned to work. After lunch the co-leader, a retired missionary, suggested that the team start working on another phase of the project 'tying iron'. The group leaped enthusiastically into the task: straightening, measuring, cutting, tying and even carrying the iron from the store to the work site three blocks away.

When that job was finished, they began carrying sand and gravel by the bucket load as well as concrete blocks to the work area.

On the fourth and fifth days both the visiting team and the Haitian workers were working together on the roof. Unfortunately, it was time to leave just as a good rapport was developed. The roof was completed the following week by the Haitian workers. Praise to the Lord of the harvest!

The group received many a 'God bless you' from the new residents of housing project.

What was really going on behind the scenes? The workers feared that they would lose their jobs because of these "interlopers." Their anxiety was probably due to the fact that the pastor of the church had laid off about half of the original crew several weeks before because there were too many workers for the size of the project.

The fact that the visiting work team was willing to do the menial labor enthusiastically and with a smile did much build the bridge of harmony and friendship between the Haitians and the visiting team.

From the notes of Herb Rogers, retired missionary serving in Haiti.

GIVING TO DO NO HARM – CASE STUDY 1

John and Sandy were SO excited to be on this short-term mission. After months of preparation, they were finally here!! Their Sunday school class was moved by their reports on the situation in the country and had raised $1,500. They asked John and Sandy to look for an opportunity to give this money to someone who would use it to bless others. John and Sandy did not mention the money to their team leader since it was a gift from their class earmarked for a special project of John and Sandy's choosing. Besides, they didn't want any personal glory from giving this gift; it was to be given quietly and without fanfare so that God would receive the honor and not their church.

John and Sandy visited an urban slum area and were deeply moved by what they saw. They were inspired by the young couple who ran a day care program for little children so that their mothers could work at the local factory for a few dollars a day. When John and Sandy found out that the couple had a dream of building a small church in the tiny open space in front of the day care, they immediately offered the $1,500 for the project. It was exactly the amount needed!

But there was more to the story. What John and Sandy did not know was that there was also a kindergarten program right next to the day care. It was funded by a different organization and run by an energetic young woman. The couple and this young woman had not been on speaking terms for several years due to a heated disagreement over how to share the limited common space. However, over the past year, with the help of some local pastors, they had begun to re-establish relationships and heal old hurts.

The new church built in the tiny shared open space changed everything. Tempers flared again as the new church building cut off the light and blocked the airflow to the kindergarten, leaving their classrooms dim and stuffy in the tropical heat. "How could you do this to my children?!" shouted the young woman to the couple. That was the last time they spoke to each other for the next three years.

From the notes of Ann Borquist, missionary.

GIVING TO DO NO HARM – CASE STUDY 2

(based on a true story)

When STM teams come without preparation, they can be an imposition on the national church. One such team came and refused to listen to the suggestions of the local pastor. In the evening after services the team was walking to a local ice cream parlor. Some of the neighborhood children were following them and one particular child appeared very adorable to a team member. The pastor asked the team member not to purchase ice cream for the child, explaining that the whole neighborhood would descend upon the team if he did.

The team member disobeyed and purchased the ice cream anyway. Soon after he handed the ice cream cone to the child, the little boy returned to the parlor with 27 other children, and more continued to arrive.

When the team saw that the other children were demanding ice cream, they became angry and began making unkind comments about the people of the country in general. It became a very ugly situation. The pastor was hurt and embarrassed. He began to dread the arrival of the next team that would arrive in three weeks. Would they be as disrespectful and rude as this team?

The children looked forward to the visits of the rich Americans. "I hope they bring toys next time," thought the little boy.

Three weeks later, the next STM team stepped off the plane…

Photo by Daniel Buttry

PACKING LIST

(* denotes carry-on item)

(? denotes items that may or may not be necessary for your trip — best to check with your hosts about what is available in the host country)

Important Documents

- Plane ticket*
- Passport with visa*
- Picture ID*
- Money*
- Money belt*
- TSA approved keys to luggage*
- Travel Insurance card*

Toiletries

- Personal prescriptions (in original containers)* Note: Many over the counter medications in the US are only available with a prescription in other countries.
- Toiletries (toothbrush*, paste*, soap, shampoo, deodorant*, razor, comb/ brush*, feminine products*). Note TSA requirements for carrying liquids.
- Contact lens products* (better to take eyeglasses if possible)
- Individual tissue packs*
- Medication for diarrhea, aspirin, band-aids, etc.*
- Water bottle* (must be empty to go through security)
- Sunglasses*
- Water purification tablets?*
- Disinfectant hand wash*
- Face masks*

Devotional/Reflection items

- Bible*
- Journal*
- Pens/pencils*
- Address list*
- Reading material*

Other good stuff

- Sunscreen
- Insect repellent
- Skin lotion & lip balm
- Sewing kit & safety pins
- Resealable plastic bags and a few plastic grocery bags
- Small laundry soap?
- Granola bars/dried fruit?*
- A pack of "Thank you Cards"
- Adapter plugs for the host country
- Flashlight & batteries?
- Wet wipes
- Camera and extra battery
- Sleeping bag & pillow or sheet and blanket?
- Travel games*
- Positive attitude*
- Sense of humor*
- Daily tote bag/backpack

- Pictures of your family*
- Postcards from home
- 6 clothespins

Ministry stuff

- Work gloves
- Work shoes
- Tools (that you can donate? Check with hosts)
- VBS materials? – toys, games, etc.
- Flexibility
- Pocket phrase book or application*
- Outline of your testimony
- Musical instrument?
- Servant's heart*
- Simple gifts for hosts
- More flexibility

Clothing

- 2 pairs of pants and/or skirts
- Long/modest shorts
- 3 – 4 cotton shirts/t-shirts
- Walking shoes
- Flip flops for shower
- Underwear
- Socks
- Church outfit & shoes
- Light towel & washcloth

- Sun hat/bandana
- Poncho/umbrella?
- Jacket/sweater
- Sweatshirt
- Modest swimsuit
- Ear plugs?
- Extra pair of glasses

NOTE: pack one change of clothes in carry-on*

NOTE: Coordinate with other team members about who will bring what. Every person does not have to have their own bottle of sunscreen, repellant, sewing kit, pocketknife, games, etc.

BOTTOM LINE: Check with your hosts on what to bring! It may be more convenient to purchase some basic items in the host country.

TEAM TRAVEL ITINERARY

Prepare an info sheet with the following items. Send the .pdf version to team members and church leaders.

1. Dates and times of departure and arrival, including names of airports

2. Note about luggage allowance

3. Lodging names and telephone numbers

4. Time zone differences

5. Notes about using ATMs or exchanging money; research currency exchange rates using this site: https://www1.oanda.com/currency/converter/

6. Note about making long distance calls (e.g. include access numbers to and from your destination country)

7. Consider using WhatsApp, Facebook Messenger or other application to communicate with loved ones.

8. Local contact person including phone number and e-mail address. This is the person you should contact in the case of an emergency.

SAMPLE DAILY SCHEDULES

LIVING OFF-SITE

6:00 a.m. Wake up

7:00 a.m. Breakfast

7:45 a.m. Devotions & reflection

8:30 a.m. Travel to project/work site

9 a.m. – 4 p.m. Work/visit ministries/VBS

4:00 p.m. Free time

6:00 p.m. Supper

7:00 p.m. Alternative time for devotions & reflection

10:30 p.m. Lights out

LIVING ON-SITE

6:00 a.m. Wake up

6:45 a.m. Devotions/Quiet time

7:15 a.m. Breakfast

8 a.m. – 1 p.m. Project/VBS

2:00 p.m. Main meal

3:00 – 5:00 p.m. Free time

5:00 – 6:00 p.m. Devotional & reflection

6:30 p.m. Evening meal

7:00 p.m. Evening Service with the host church

TIPS FOR MANAGING JET LAG

Before and during the flight:

1. Eat lots of fruits and vegetables for two days before you leave and three days after you arrive at your destination. Eat pasta or rice the night before your flight.

2. Avoid heavy meals for 24 hrs. before your flight (e.g. hunks of meat, fatty or fried food).

3. About 48 hours before your flight, set your watch to the time of your destination country. Make sure this isn't your alarm clock! Begin to adjust your daily schedule to match that of your destination country.

4. Drink plenty of water and fruit juices, especially during the flight. Avoid caffeine and alcoholic drinks. Also, walk around the plane once every hour on long flights.

After you arrive:

1. After you arrive, spend as much time as possible outdoors in natural lighting. This will help your body to naturally adjust to the time change.

2. Make a special effort to get plenty of exercise in the first couple of days after arrival.

3. Count on your body taking about one day to adjust to each hour of difference in time. So, for example, it will probably take about two to three days for your body to adjust to a three-hour time difference between your home and the destination country.

4. If jet lag is more than six hours, for the first one to two days, do not drive a vehicle or engage in any activities that require a high level of alertness or precision (e.g. medical work, conflict mediation, equipment testing or maintenance, etc.)

TIPS FOR SPEAKING THROUGH AN INTERPRETER

1. Speak slowly and in short sentences. Be kind to your translator!

2. Use ordinary, easily understood English. Avoid using jargon, slang or clichés. ("I was wiped out after the hike." "Do you want to hang out with me?")

3. Steer clear of jokes. Humor sometimes translates very differently in another language!

4. Remember that your 20-minute sermon will translate into at least a 40-minute message and might even go to an hour!

5. Avoid organizing your testimony or sermon using alliteration in English which doesn't translate into another language, e.g. Prayer, Promise and Provision becomes "Doa, janji [and] ketentuan" in the language of Indonesia.

6. Double check that the key word or phrase in the host translation matches the point you are making. For example, one person based their whole message and their sermon illustrations on "how we walk" as believers. However, the translation made no mention of the word "walk"; rather, it used the phrase "to live."

7. If you quote verses, make sure that the verse in the host country language is the same chapter and verse as in the English or Spanish version you are using. (Numbering of Bible verses was started in the 16th century. This was after the Bible was already translated into a number of languages. Therefore, in some areas there might be a slight difference in notation, especially in the Psalms and some chapters in the New Testament).

PHOTOS AND VIDEO TIPS

1. Check with your hosts (pastors or global servants) about any taboos regarding photography.

2. Discern the purpose of photos you want to take.

3. Be sensitive to the timing of your picture taking. Avoid disturbing worship services, especially prayer meetings. In some areas, photographing or videotaping a worship service is strictly prohibited. In a country where Christians face persecution or discrimination, showing their picture back home or posting it on the internet could result in serious harm.

4. Take photos of PEOPLE. Take photos of daily activities like cooking, shopping, farming, relaxing, going to school. Try for candid shots rather than posed pictures. Flora and fauna are nice, but your focus should be on the people you have come to serve and learn from.

   - your host families

   - the host pastor(s)

   - the global servants

   - the people you are working with

5. Make sure you focus on the FACES of people. Check out the background – does it provide a good contrast or is it distracting?

6. Close-up shots of one or two people are far more interesting than a group shot of 57 tiny looking people in front of the school.

7. Make sure the sun is behind you if you are taking pictures outside. If indoors, be sure to use a flash and get CLOSE to your subject.

8. If you would like pictures of famous buildings or landscapes, buy a postcard. If you must take a picture yourself, make sure a team member is in your photo. Get close enough to take a picture of their face/shoulders with your fabulous scene in the background.

9. Keep a record of each shot you take! Note the who, what, where, when of the picture.

Send copies of a few of your best photos with a short explanation to the Short-Term Missions at International Ministries
volunteers@internationalministries.org